Jesus Christ is my Heartmender

Poetry by
Connie Hinks Porcher

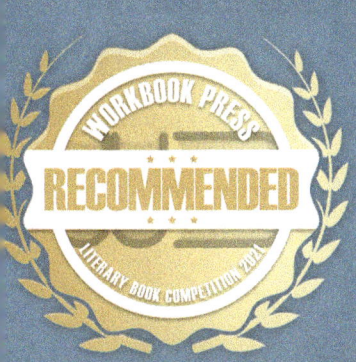

Copyright @2021 by Connie Porcher

All rights reserved. No part of this book may be reproduced in any form or by any electronic or mechanical means, including information storage and retrieval systems, without permission in writing from the publisher, except by reviewers, who may quote brief passages in a review.

This publication contains the opinions and ideas of its author. It is intended to provide helpful and informative material on the subjects addressed in the publication. The author and publisher specifically disclaim all responsibility for any liability, loss or risk, personal or otherwise, which is incurred as a consequence, directly or indirectly, of the use and application of any of the contents of this book.

WORKBOOK PRESS LLC
187 E Warm Springs Rd,
Suite B285, Las Vegas, NV 89119, USA

Website: https://workbookpress.com/
Hotline: 1-888-818-4856
Email: admin@workbookpress.com

Ordering Information:
Quantity sales. Special discounts are available on quantity purchases by corporations, associations, and others.
For details, contact the publisher at the address above.

Library of Congress Control Number:
ISBN-13: 978-1-954753-95-2 (Paperback Version)
978-1-954753-96-9 (Digital Version)

REV. DATE: 09/04/2021

Dedication....to all who have meant so much...

*For Fulfilling Faith....*First and foremost, this book is dedicated to Jesus Christ, the Master Heartmender...*I give you all honor and glory for your abiding presence in my life and your gracious gift of the poetry and the meaningfulness of the message that you have provided. My Heavenly Father, Savior, Counselor, Guide and Friend...you, Lord are the one I turn to when life is full...be it joy or sorrow. I love you Lord. Thank you for guiding me on this leg of my eternal journey. My prayer Lord is that you will use the heart-borne words within this book, to encourage each reader and mend the heart-torn among us. I pray Father that the readers find peace, joy and contentment, but most of all your forgiveness and salvation.* **"For this is the day the Lord has made. I will rejoice and be glad in it."**

For Devoted Family....The love of my life is Tom...Tom you have walked beside me in good times and in other times for nearly 50 years. I give you my respect and honor your godly influence in my life and especially in my writing. When poems needed airing, you patiently listened; when the fulfillment of my dream for this book needed uplifting, you were there prodding me on to progress. So, dear husband, I dedicate this book to you, with a grateful heart. One of the dearest blessings is our lovely daughter, Lori. She is not only beautiful outside but inside as well. To you, daughter of my heart, I dedicate this book. To Randy, our son, I thank God for you and the love you have shown your Daddy and me throughout the years. We have shared tears of joy and sorrow, but through them all we have become even closer and stronger than ever. In my notebook I discovered something you wrote many years ago. It is profound and deeply insightful-- "Tear filled eyes will never dry until the light shines from within." Thank you, son.

*For Loving Friends....*God knows my heart and is so good to have surrounded me with so many faithful friends over so many years. I cherish each tender heart and your thoughtful ways. Your truthfulness, forgiveness, trustworthy participation in my life have given me joy beyond expression. Each of you have filled me with your love and caring. My desire is that each one of you share Jesus the Lord of your life with all who cross your path. I am so very proud to be your friend and dedicate these poems to you with all my heart.

For Faithful Assistants: I so appreciate the helpful suggestions, comments, and encouragement you have provided me. Debi Hassler, what a friend you have been. You listened and helped me more than you know. To my granddaughter, Lacey Scott for editing this book. You are my joy. And to Tim Boyle, who patiently gave me sound advice and contributed much through his own writing experience. Each one of you has helped bring this book to it's conclusion and I thank you all.

Table of Contents

God's Instrument 01

Genesis 02

Moses 03

With Wings Like Eagles 04

Silent Weeper 05

Be Still and Know 06

Salvation! Hallelujah! 07

Your Heart's Door 08

The Glory of the Son 09

Tear Catcher 10

Seeds Of Love 11

The Man From Galilee 12

Our Days Are Numbered 13

This Is Your Coronation Day 14

Trees Along A Riverbank 15

Jesus Is My Fortress And My Rock 16

Come, Oh Lord 17

The Counselor 18

In The Morning 19

The Joy of Sorrow 20

Nobody's Child 21

His Name Is Wonderful *22*

Mom *24*

For The Love Of My Family, ...*25*

Love Of My Life *26*

I Love You, I Understand *27*

Sweet Sixteen *28*

My Son *29*

Grandchildren *30*

Friends Are Friends Forever *32*

Friends *33*

Building Bridges *34*

Gifts From A Loving Heart *35*

The Gift Of Love *36*

Our Greatest Friend *37*

FAITH

1982

God's Instrument

The words I write are not my own--I'm just God's instrument.
He lays the message on my heart. With pen in hand I print.
And if the words bring pleasant thoughts to dance upon your mind.
The one to thank is God above, if you will be so kind.

For in His loving plan He knew the words I'd like to say,
And brought them forth, out of my heart, to share with you today.
I want for each of you to know I value much your friendship,
And treasure every moment spent developing a kinship.

Just talking every now and then and knowing that you care,
Has filled my heart with sunshine, as with me you have shared.
Sometimes it only takes a smile, or just a friendly touch,
To make the shadows fly away…..it really isn't much.

And yet, the kind words we could say are locked within our hearts.
We hang onto them tightly, not letting them depart.
If only we could open up and give our love away,
It would come bounding back again to brighten up our day.

So let's follow God's example, spreading sunshine all around,
'Cause darkness cannot stay for long where God's love-light abounds.
Perhaps when you and I begin to give our love away,
Each day through out the whole year long, will be a blessed day.

"For God so loved the world that He gave His only Son so that anyone who believes in Him shall not perish but have eternal life."
John 3:16

1981

Genesis

Genesis, book of beginnings. Praise to Almighty God.
He spoke the words, "Let there be light," and so began the day and night.
Day number two gave us the sky and all the seas below.
Dry land emerged out from the sea. He called it earth; it grew a tree.
Thus ended day number three.
A bright and shining light He placed up in the sky so blue.
One for the day He called the sun, a smaller one, the moon.
Day number four was now complete, but there would be more soon.
Into the waters called the seas went creatures large and small.
The fish and other living things would live there, one and all.
Every kind of bird that fly's would fill the big blue sky.
All this was done in one day's time thus ending number five.
And now to bring forth animals to walk upon the land.
The cattle and the wildlife and reptiles for the sand.
But still one thing was missing , in God's great master plan.
Male and female, in His image, made only as God can.
Day six was ended now at last, for God had finished every task.
Thus, the heavens and the earth complete, all the host of them.
And on the seventh day God rested from all the work He'd done.
He blessed this day and hallowed it. "It's very good, yes, every bit."
Creation began so perfectly, without a single flaw.
Beauty was upon the earth in everything He saw.
But soon sin entered in because man broke God's Holy law.

*"When God began creating the heavens and the earth,
the earth was at first a shapeless, chaotic mass,
with the Spirit of God brooding over the dark vapors." Genesis 1:*

1982

Moses

Because his faith was very small when God called out to Moses,
He was afraid to stand alone and so a friend was chosen.
To walk along beside of him and lend a helping hand,
For Moses had not faith enough on God alone to stand.
God knew that His great power was sufficient for each task.
Moses did not need an Aaron, but God gave him what he asked.
And soon the problems mounted up…..the multitudes did laugh,
When Aaron, Moses' chosen one, had made the golden calf.
In anger, Moses broke the stone that carried God's Holy laws,
For the friend he wanted to stand with him had become to him a flaw.
If only he had stood alone and trusted God, you see,
He wouldn't have to suffer this intense humility.
All things together work for good, that is God's way, we know.
He took that tiny seed of faith and began to make it grow.
For Moses loved his mighty God and turned to Him in prayer.
To speak to God of many things and found Him waiting there.
Planted in a willing heart, the seed of faith did grow,
Though thorns of tribulation made the growing very slow.
Eventually, friend Moses, became a humble man.
He learned to trust in God alone and on His Word to stand.
His story is recorded in God's Word for you and me.
That we might learn what Moses learned; trust God eternally.

"The Lord is my strength , my song, and my salvation.
He is my God and I will praise Him." Exodus 15:2

1981

With Wings Like Eagles

To dwell in peace and safety, there is only one sure way.
Through Jesus Christ as Savior. Call on Him today.

He'll be your fortress and your guide. He knows the way, that's true.
Under His wings you'll safely hide. His mercies are ever new.

Your fears He'll calm so quietly. Sweet rest He'll gently bring,
When troubles high around you soar He'll make your heart to sing.

He loves you very, very much. On this you can depend.
And if you trust Him fully, eternity with Him you'll spend.

*"But they that wait upon the Lord shall renew their strength.
They shall mount up with wings like eagles;
they shall run and not be weary;
they shall walk and not faint." Isaiah 40:31*

1985

Silent Weeper

From the heart of a Silent Weeper tears of anguish swiftly flow,
Kept inside by a wall of pride, but only the Weeper knows.

For even though the pains go deep and pierce the aching soul,
In silence and in quietness, the hurt remains untold.

Locked within the agony of many broken hearts,
The secrets held so deep within, will not soon depart

Instead, a shadow will appear, a victim you will be.
The person others think you are, you'll surely never see.

For when we wear a mask each day to cover up our fears,
And put a smile upon our lips, and camouflage our tears,

Instead of feeling free within, new prison walls we build….
The pain we tried to keep locked out, our heart it now has filled.

There is but one way to be free, to end this awful plight,
To put an end to your despair and make things turn out right.

But, first you must confess your sins of selfishness and pride
And open up your broken heart; no longer secrets hide.

And when, with courage, you express your heart about the matter,
The pent-up tears will heal your heart. Your prison walls will shatter.

Jesus Christ, The Son Of God, is reaching out to you.
HE alone can understand and make your life brand new.

HE knows the sorrow in your soul, HIS pain is even deeper.
He died, alone, upon the cross, for the heart of a Silent Weeper.

"… Weeping may go on all night, but in the morning there is joy."
Psalm 30:5

1991

Be Still and Know

Be still and know my child that I am God.
The paths you take I have already trod.

Here, take my hand and walk along with me.
You're not alone, but safe as you can be.

I know that in your valley it is dark.
So very, very hard to find your way.

Remember when they nailed me to the cross,
And darkness came, without a single ray

Of Light or Hope? I hung there as a man,
Not God. It was my Father's plan.

I felt the pain, the searing pain.
My heart was crying too….

When suddenly I realized
That anguish was for you.

For then I knew that when you hurt,
You could come to me.

Together, hand in hand, we'll walk
Out of that dark valley.

I Am The Way, I Am The Light.
There is no darkness here.

The sun is shining brightly now.
The way is very clear.

So, Be Still, and know, my child, that I am God.
The paths you take I have already trod.

"Stand silent! Know that I am God!
I will be honored by every nation in the world."
Psalm 46:10

1981

Salvation! Hallelujah!

Salvation! Hallelujah!
His praises will I sing.
I'll shout it to those round about.
Oh, let the joy bells ring!

Oh, listen all ye people
To what God will do for you.
He will give you peace and safety,
Whether Gentile or Jew.

He is the mighty Savior,
Prince of peace and counselor.
His life He gave, that you might live.
How could you ask for more?

Accept Him now, the time is right.
Oh, please do not delay.
Salvation, Hallelujah!
It could be yours today!

"The Lord is my light and my salvation; whom shall I fear?"
Psalm 27:1

1975

Your Heart's Door

If I could tell you in such a way,
That you would understand.
The thoughts within my heart that lie.
It really would be grand.

But, since they lie so deep within
A heart that's filled with love.
I'll simply, quietly, trust them to
The One who is above.

I'll ask Him if He would not mind.
To speed them on their way,
That they might enter your heart's door.
This very blessed day.

I'll ask the Holy Spirit,
Which is His specialty,
To breathe the words from me to you
In perfect harmony.

You see, because we're such good friends
And everything is in His hand.
I know He'll take my thoughts to you
And you will understand.

*"Look! I have been standing at the door and I am constantly knocking.
If anyone hears me calling him and opens the door,
I will come in and fellowship with him and he with me."
Revelation 3:20*

2009

The Glory of the Son

It was the dawning of the morning,
Just at first light.
The beginning of a new day.
Oh, what a sight.

The sun was peeking
Over the hill.
The earth was very quiet
And everything was still.

It reminded me of
Another Son,
Who filled the earth with light.
But He had only just begun.

The Son of God's presence
Brightened up the sky,
Bringing tears of His Majesty
Falling from my eyes.

His glory and grandeur
Shown round about.
Oh, I wanted to hear all the earth
Begin to shout.

To let the world know,
That He is the Son.
It was He who created
The glorious rising sun.

That spoke to my heart
As I saw what He had done
And I knew that the glory
Belonged to the Son.

Yes, I knew that the glory
Belonged to the Son.

*And now--all glory to Him who alone is God,
who saves us through Jesus Christ our Lord;
yes, splendor and majesty, all power and authority are
His from the beginning;
His they are and His they evermore shall be. Amen.
Jude 1:25*

1981

Tear Catcher

Daily we see them as we pass on the street.
Hearts that are breaking in many we meet.
Arms that are heavy, knees that are weak.
Bearing great burdens of which they can't speak.

Eyes that no longer sparkle with joy,
Everything shattered like yesterday's toy.
Hearing no laughter, no smile do they see;
Searching for happiness, "Where can it be?"

No time to listen, too busy to hear,
The weeping at midnight when no one is near.
A kind word, a smile, to show that we care
Would lighten, considerably, the burden they bear.

But, still we pass by, unaware of the pain,
Thinking only this moment of what we can gain…..
Until the day comes when our own heart breaks in two,
And we know from experience the hurt others went through.

Perhaps it's a lesson each one of us needs.
Perhaps it's the way God plants His Love seeds…..
In the soil of deep sorrow, watered by tears,
So our lives will be fruitful, and not wasted years.

God treasures the drops from our eyes that are shed.
In a bottle He keeps them His Holy Word said.
Perchance He needs helpers to hear when they fall.
Lord, please make tear catchers of us, one and all.

*"You have seen me tossing and turning through the night.
You have collected all my tears and preserved them in your bottle!
You have recorded every one in your book."
Psalm 56:8*

1988

Seeds Of Love

The message spread across the land, but not the way you think.
It's words were written on a heart, but not with pen and ink.

No lace or pretty flowers decorate this valentine,
Still the love it held within, just made it fairly shine.

I still can hear it's message ringing softly in my ears.
"I love you, yes, I love you," whispered gently through His tears.

It was not made with paper, not with ribbons or with lace.
You could not find it at a store, or buy it anyplace.

Perhaps you've guessed the truth by now, even though I've just begun.
God gave the world a valentine, when He gave the world His Son.

Upon the cross was nailed a man. Christ Jesus was His Name.
The sin of all the world was placed upon His humble frame.

He suffered for us on that cross, and gladly bore our shame.
While King of Kings and Lord of Lords. He rightfully could claim.

Yes, on a hill there stands a cross, and on that cross a man.
Inside the man, a broken heart, who kept God's holy plan.

And from that broken heart came love; it's goodness ever flowing.
And seeds of love were spread about…soon they started growing.

For in each heart where love is sown. And in His special time.
That love, when shared between two hearts will make a valentine.
And now you know the story true, of the world's first valentine.
Sent with love from heaven, to your heart and to mine.

*"There are three things that remain--faith, hope,
and love--and the greatest of these is love."
I Corinthians 13:13*

2010

The Man From Galilee

Have you heard the old, old story of the Man from Galilee?
Who gave His life upon the cross. He died for you and me.

We only need to ask Him to forgive our sins, you see,
'Cause He's the Man from Galilee who sets the captives free.

He is the Way, the Truth, the Life. Your Savior He can be.
When you put your trust in Christ alone and worship His Majesty.

He is more than just our Savior. He wants to be our Lord.
The fragrance of His sweet perfume, cannot be ignored.

For where your footsteps lead you, He will go before.
He'll lead, He'll guide and walk beside. Alone you'll be no more.

So remember the old, old story of the Man from Galilee,
'Cause He's the one who gave His life. He died for you and me.

He is the King of glory and He will always be,
Our only hope to spend our days with Him eternally.

So won't you please consider who He's asking you to be?
Then you can walk forever with the Man from Galilee.

"Jesus told him, "I am the Way--yes, and the Truth and the Life.
No one can get to the Father except by means of me....."
John 14:6

1994

Our Days Are Numbered

Teach us Lord to number our days,
Our weeks, our months, our years.
That we may apply our hearts to wisdom,
Gaining strength through our sorrows and fears.

The days come quickly, one after another.
Each one of them numbered by God.
We're given a few, His will to do,
Then our bodies return to the sod.

Help us, dear Lord, to carefully choose
Your will for our lives each day.
Wherever we go, whatever we do,
Whether at work or at play.

To do as you bid each day of our lives
Your mercy and grace are free.
To be whatever you want me to be,
Well, that will be glory for me!

*"Teach us to number our days and recognize how few they are;
help us to spend them as we should."
Psalm 90:12*

1980

This Is Your Coronation Day

What fools the nations are
To rage against the Lord.
Listen, while there still is time
Oh, listen to His Word.

He is the ruler of the world
His throne will never fall.
Oh, Kings and rulers of the earth,
Come, hear Him, one and all.

"Let us break His chains" they say
"And end this slavery to God'"
He merely laughs at all their plans.
Then rebukes them with His rod.

But to His Son, Jesus the Christ,
He gladly crowns Him King!
Serve Him with reverent, holy fear…..
And peace and joy He'll bring.

"Lord, be exalted above the highest heavens!
Show your glory high above the earth."
Psalm 57:5

1980

Trees Along A Riverbank

To be most blessed by God, there is a way the Psalmist said.
The man who finds His favor will by His word be led.

In the way of sinners he'll not walk, or stand, or sit, but in God's law he'll meditate and find great joy in it.
Planted by the rivers of water, He shall be like a tree.
Mighty, sheltering, bountiful that's how his life will be.

Alone, afraid, no never, because he knows the One
Who gave him life, freedom from strife. That man is God's great Son.

So if you're seeking to be blessed, and you need a path to trod.

Take Jesus as your Savior. He's the only way to God.

"They are like trees along a river bank bearing luscious fruit each season without fail.

Their leaves shall never wither, and all they do shall prosper."
Psalm 1:3

1980

Jesus Is My Fortress And My Rock

Silently before the Lord I stand.
Knowing I'll be rescued by His hand.

Should I be afraid or should I fear,
Worry, or resort to shedding tears?

Oh no, He is my Fortress and my Rock.
And I know beside me He does walk.

He is loving, kind and rewards each one
According to the work we've done.

To wait on God is to be strong.
To trust in Him is never wrong.

Whether we are great or small,
Salvation is His gift to all.

But first on Him we must believe,
And then by faith His truth receive.

"The Lord is my fort where I can enter and be safe;
no one can follow me in and slay me.
He is a rugged mountain where I can hide;
He is my Savior, a rock where none can reach me,
and a tower of safety...."
Psalm 18:2

1980

Come, Oh Lord

My weeping He has heard,
As on my bed I lay.
Tears are falling from my eyes,
All night and through the day.

You workers of iniquity
Quickly depart from me,
For I am His and He is mine.
And He will set me free.

For soon the sun
Will brightly shine, and I will smile once more.
He will open wide the heavenly gate.
That's what I'm waiting for.

"Come, O Lord, and make me well. In your kindness save me."
Psalm 6:4

1976

The Counselor

With heart of compassion and words of good cheer,
He listens and listens and really does hear.

As people whose lives are filled with deep pain
Unload and unburden and pour out their shame.

Their lives have been broken and shattered by sin.
They try to repair it but where to begin?

His counsel is wise and sure to succeed
As he brings God's word to bear on their deeds.

If only, if only, we would learn to obey.
Our hearts would be mended and joy fill our day.

But so often we listen and don't really hear,
Our hearts we have hardened though the path is so clear.

Sometimes when the burdens are too heavy to bear
He reminds them that Jesus still loves and still cares.

If we will but trust Him he'll teach and he'll guide.
We'll never be losers with God on our side.

He counsels them wisely, "hang in there," says he.
"With you in your problem, that's where I will be."

The tears they come often.....It's not strange that they do.
So he hands them a tissue and says, "I cry too."

So thank you, dear pastor for sharing your love.
I know God is pleased as He sees from above.

And now as I bring these words to an end,
I'd just like to say thank you counselor, thank you friend!

"get all the advice you can and be wise the rest of your life."
Proverbs 19:20

1981

In The Morning

Early in the morning light, before the sun has risen.
You're waiting by the Pearly gates to hear from those You've chosen.

Fellowship is sweet indeed when shared with God above.
He hears His children when they pray and surrounds them with His love.

So, carefully evaluate the things that take your time.
And give to Him a moment while the day is in it's prime.

Do not wait for night to come and sleep to fill your soul.
Before you talk to Jesus or He cannot make you whole.

*"Each morning I will look to you in heaven
and lay my requests before you, praying earnestly."
Psalm 5:3*

1981

The Joy of Sorrow

In the midst of deepest pain, when your heart is near to breaking.
And all around is mass confusion, and your world is really shaking.
Where do you run? Where do you hide, when hope has gone and love has died?

There is no place on this great earth where sadness doesn't touch.

It's part of every human life and it gives us, oh, so much.
How can that be, your soul might say. There is a way.

There is a way. In the heart of every man is found a vacancy,
created by the hand of God and filled by only He.
When the troubles in your life begin to overwhelm,
turn your eyes upon the one who is seated at the helm.

He'll turn your darkness into light, bring sunshine out of rain.
Your sorrow He will turn to joy and peace will come through pain.

*"....when their sorrow was turned to gladness
and their mourning into happiness."
Esther 9:2*

1990

Nobody's Child

Silently she stands there waiting, as from her eye there slowly falls a tear.
Waiting for those words "I love you," spoken by a voice she'll never hear.
Alone, apart, he bravely stands watching the world go by.
Afraid to open his heart's door, 'cause big boys shouldn't cry

I'm nobody's child. I'm nobody's girl.
Nobody loves me, and nobody will.

I'm nobody's child. I'm nobody's boy.
Nobody loves me. I'm nobody's joy.

Oh, when will we listen, when will we share,
The heartaches and burdens our little ones bear?
The pain on their face is so easy to see,
But only if we are on bended knee.
For from that position as we talk to our God.
He will help us remember the path we have trod.
And those childhood memories will come to the fore,
And we'll feel what it's like to be five once more.
And maybe, just maybe, as we see through their eyes,
We will take off our masks and remove our disguise.
We'll reach out and touch them and teach them to smile,
And show them, at last, they are Somebody's child.

I'm Somebody's child, I'm Somebody's girl.
Somebody loves me and He always will!
I'm Somebody's child. I'm Somebody's boy.
Somebody loves me. I'm Somebody's joy!

*"And any of you who welcomes a little child like this
because you are mine, is welcoming me and caring for me."
Matthew 18: 5Esther 9:2*

1981

His Name Is Wonderful

What a wonderful, glorious, excellent Name…..
Far greater than any on earth.
His glory outreaches the heavens.
There is none to compare to His worth.

He is the Lord, and Master of all,
Though some scarcely know His name.
And yet one day, their knee will bow,
As His children He comes to claim.

Oh, listen, dear people, while there is still time,
To the message He brings your way.
His death, His burial and resurrection,
Believe it…..be saved today!

He loves you more than you can know,
His words are ever true.
He came to bring new life, new hope,
And He did it just for you.

Jesus Christ is a wonderful Savior,
Glorious, excellent, too.
Everyone can come to Him,
And He's waiting …..just for you!

"There is salvation in no one else!
Under all heaven there is no other name for men
to call upon to save them."
Acts 4:12

FAMILY

1988

Mom

Memories of yesterday are patterned on my mind.
Another time, another place--the pieces are hard to find.

I see her face, her gentle smile, the gnarled and wrinkled hands.
Her twinkling eyes, her dimpled cheeks…..all grains of shimmering sand.

Yes, God took her up to heaven, the one I loved so true.
But He has given her back to me through my beautiful minds eye view.

And who, this lovely soul might be. I'll tell you if I may.
She is the mother who gave me life, and I cherish my thoughts today.

Her meek and gentle spirit. Her quiet, thoughtful ways.
Her listening ears and hearing heart gave meaning to my days.

She was a real example to her children, one and all.
And to this day each one of us, see her standing brave and tall.

She taught us that it's wise to live our lives for one another.
She gave us all she had to give, and I say, "Thank you, Mother."

I've grown a lot since you went away, but more growing I must do.
God's grace I pray, one day will change me, so I can be like you.

*"Charm can be deceptive, and beauty doesn't last,
but a woman who fears and reverences God shall be greatly praised."
Proverbs 31:30*

2011

For The Love Of My Family,

My Daddy was born a long time ago, 1890 was the year.
In those days children were raised with a firm hand.
His expectations very clear.
Until the 8th grade, he did go to school but work he had to do.
The rest of his life he worked very hard because it was all he knew.

His work took him many places when he became a man.
Most of the time he ran a dragline, building canals and dams.
He raised twelve children, doing the best he could.
He provided food for our table just as he knew he should.

He married my mother when she was twenty-one.
And soon the children born to them entered the world one by one.
One of my brothers, born in a hospital. At home, all the rest were born.
Six girls and three boys to them they gave life,
in those days that was the norm.

Our own personalities took form as we grew.
Disagreements we had as most families do.
But still underneath is a love that will last
Time is moving too quickly and soon will be past.

Our time on this earth is too brief we each say.
So we make the best of each special day.
Five sisters I'm blessed with, not everyone so.
They're a part of my heart wherever I go.

Many things I have learned from each one you see
Your examples are very precious to me.
Six have been married fifty years and more.
But then, no ones keeping the years, nor the score.

Tom and I, in our 48th year,
That milestone to reach with the one I hold dear.
To my nieces and nephews, and there are quite a few.
I long to see you much more than I do.

I want for you all to know that I love you
It's easy to say because it is true.

*"O Lord, I will praise you with all my heart,
and tell everyone about the marvelous things you do."
Psalms 9:1*

Love Of My Life

There's only one man in my life who means the world to me.
He is the strong and silent type, but his love is plain to see.

He's always so dependable, so fine in every way.
The feelings held inside my heart can't find the words to say.

If you knew him the way I do you would see a great big heart,
Who has given all he's got to us right from the very start.

How can I tell you husband dear, that I appreciate you,
That I love, admire and respect the man inside of you.

Days come and then the days are gone….too quickly I might add.
In the beginning you were mine alone, but now you are a "Dad".

A mighty fine father you are indeed, no man could ever be better.
Because as a dad you truly have lived up to every letter.

Some people think their happiness lies in the riches money can buy. But my wealth comes through being loved by my one and only guy!

He may be short of stature, but to me he's ten feet tall.
It's really what's inside that counts, now isn't it, after all?

Inside he is a gentle man who never asks for much.
Only a hug and a kiss or two, and sometimes a tender touch.

Oh, love of my life, you are the wisest of men.
I've loved you for always, but I'll tell you again.

I love you, Sweetheart.

*"Be delighted with the Lord. Then
He will give you all your heart's desires."
Psalm 37:4*

1975

I Love You, I Understand

When I failed him, he didn't criticize and condemn.

He only spoke with tender compassion as he said,
"I love you, I understand."
When I turned my back upon him,
he didn't revile me, or wallow in self pity.

No, he only took my hand and whispered, "I love you, I understand."

Ah, yes, but what about the times I ignore him;
when I fail to speak to him….Oh, what about then?
He gently wraps his arms close about me, and tenderly speaks,
"I love you, I understand."

Why, then, Oh Lord, when others fail me, why must I condemn them?
Why can't I speak those words, "I love you, I understand?"

Why, Father, when they ignore me, when they choose not to listen,
not to speak, why can't my heart say, "I love you, I understand?"

Oh, Father God, teach me your forgiveness, your never-ending love,
and when the time comes and I'm unable….
please speak those words through me.
"I love you, I understand."

*"….But you are a God of forgiveness, always ready to pardon,
gracious and merciful, slow to become angry,
and full of love and mercy….."
Nehemiah 9:17b*

1979

Sweet Sixteen

The beauty of a diamond. The sparkle of the dew.
The lilies in their snow white robes cannot compare with you.
The beauty of your countenance. The sparkle in your eyes.
The purity of character within your person lies.
Only God can give true beauty for it comes from deep within,
When a woman learns to trust in God and give her life to Him.
He tells us, if we would be wise, to fear and trust in Him.
To look above and seek His love. Yes, that's where we begin.
The fragrance of the sweetest rose in an exquisite vase,
Can never match the sweet perfume of God's Great Matchless Grace.
For when you wear His fragrance and the sweetness of His Spirit.
Everyone will be the richer, for they can see and hear it.
You cannot hide the beauty of a life that's hid with God.
Others will be quite aware of the pathways you have trod.
You've grown into a woman and you are a joy to me.
You have a lifetime waiting to be what God wants you to be.
Seek ye first His Kingdom, and pray only for His will.
He will guide your footsteps and your cup of joy He'll fill.
Each time you wear these precious gems, may you remember this…..
You, also, are a precious jewel, and you belong to Him.
We love you, daughter, Sweet Sixteen, and cherish you forever.
May these diamonds be a reminder of a love that none can sever!

"As far as God is concerned there is a sweet,
wholesome fragrance in our lives.
It is the fragrance of Christ within us,
an aroma to both the saved and the unsaved all around us."
2 Corinthians 2:15

1980

My Son

He is the strong and silent type. His words are very few.
He dreams great dreams and schemes great schemes.
There's nothing he can't do.
The important things in life, my son are not the things you do,
But rather what you are that counts…..the part hidden from our view.
It's caring and it's loving and giving what you can,
To make this world a better place for every living man.
Sometimes we are impatient to hurry on our way.
We want to grow, we want to know and we want it all today!
But son, there is a day ahead when your dreams will all come true.
And you will be a wiser man, if you'll wait for them to come to you.
Fools rush in where angels fear to tread, someone so rightly said.
The wise are those who daily wait for God to weave the thread.
For you see, He has the blueprint and all the tools we need,
To put our life together and make it beautiful indeed.
He is the Master Architect, with a perfect plan in mind.
Just ask Him for direction, then seek and ye shall find.
Some days the sun will brightly shine. Some days are filled with rain.
We wouldn't know what happiness is, without a little pain.
Life is a combination of pleasure, joy and sadness.
Each one who lives will have his share of goodness and of badness.
You are no longer a child, my son. You've grown into a man.
And proud I am to see that smile that says, "I can, I can!"
I believe in you my dearest son, and I know you will succeed,
Because you have a great big heart always giving to those in need.

*"My son, never forget the things I've taught you. If you want a long
and satisfying life, closely follow my instructions. Never forget to be
truthful and kind. Hold these virtues tightly.
Write them deep within your heart."
Proverbs 3:1-6*

2011

Grandchildren

I dreamed I would be a Grandma, because it's plain to see,
That they would be a special gift from the hand of God to me.
And sure enough, my dreams came true, when the time was right,
They came wrapped in blue.

One by one, joy after joy, boy, after boy, after boy, after boy!
Zachary, Jachin, Colin and Drew,
With bright shining faces, twinkling eyes, too.
Typical boys playing ball, climbing trees;
Scratches on elbows, and skinned up knees.

In pink this time, He sent me our girls and life was sublime.
Two lovely blessings, Lacey and Sable,
Wearing cute dresses, two more at the table.
Sparkles and spangles, ribbons and lace,
Lizards and frogs, all over the place.
I thought that six would be the end, but one more boy
He decided to send.

A bouncing boy, now a young man. Derrek, a special part of God's plan.
If another He sent, would they wear pants or a dress?
What would He give me? How much would He bless?

And wouldn't you know, He gave me a girl.
Grandchildren keeping my life in a whirl.
She's adorable, sweet, and beautiful too.
Maelonni, just now, I am speaking of you.

And then I was sure that completed my joys,

But God wasn't finished, for two little boys.....
Given to us on Angel's wings, my heart couldn't help but sing.

Malachi and Mason, brothers they are,
Like two little lightning bugs in a jar!
Their hugs and their kisses fill me with delight.
The toys that they scatter, oh what a sight!

I love you so much, you're each one unique.
I will support your plans, whatever you seek.
And when you are grown, and out on your own,
Just remember that I am as near as the phone!

"An old man's grandchildren are his crowning glory.
A child's glory is his father."
Proverbs 17:6

FRIENDS

1984

Friends Are Friends Forever

Friends are friends forever when the Lord's the Lord of them.
A friend will stand up for you and be faithful to the end.
A friend will help when times are tough. Their heart will empathize.
They care about your every need; their counsel is so wise.
Today they laugh and bring you joy and share your happiness.
Tomorrow they will cry with you when your hurt you can't express.
A friend will always be there. They will never give up on you.
No matter how you think or act, no matter what you do.
It's great to have that kind of friend to share your hopes and dreams;
To bind your wounds and heal your heart, yes,
that's what friendship means.
But even more importantly, we each must learn to be,
That kind of friend to others, so Jesus in us they'll see.
For if we want to have true friends, who will share our joy and pain,
We must learn first to be one. We have so much to gain.
Love is the force that binds our hearts. It's ours to freely share.
So, let's reach out and touch a life and show someone we care.
For if we give our love away and if we start today.
A friendship may begin right now and never pass away.
Remember, loves for always. It will never, never end.
And friends are friends forever, when the Lord's the Lord of them.

*"There are "friends" who pretend to be friends, but there is a friend
who sticks closer than a brother." Proverbs 18:24*

1980

Friends

Friends come and friends go, like the showers of Spring.
For a moment we're warmed by the sunshine they bring.
Their stay is so brief; they linger a while.
One day they are gone, leaving only their smile.
Occasionally we're privileged with friendships so true.
Just now I am speaking of friends like you.
Sometimes there's a feeling, right from the start,
Of loving and caring…..it comes from the heart.
And it stays and it lingers long after they're gone.
Because into your heart they have brought a new song.
You can carry the melody of their laughter with you.
Their tears and their pain, well, that's beautiful, too.
True friends, like the seedlings planted in Spring,
Are nurtured by kindness and thoughtful things.
On warm Summer days the relationship grows
Until it has the fragrance of life's sweetest rose.
The colors of Autumn bring out the rare beauty.
As the friendship matures; it's a joy…..not a duty.
And when Winter comes, with its frost and its snows.
We will count all our blessings, while the cold winds blow.
For no matter the day, nor the year, nor the season.
I'm grateful to God…..my true friends are the reason.

"A true friend is always loyal,
and a brother is born to help in time of need."
Proverbs 17:17

1979

Building Bridges

Some people say Jesus loves and He cares,
But their lives are self-centered, they take without giving.
But true love, God's love, gives without taking,
And that's what makes life worth the living.

God only has few on the pathway of life,
Who mend broken hearts everyday,
And you, my friend, are one of the few,
Who pick up the stones and throws them away,
And sees only what lies underneath.

Some people build bridges of concrete and wood,
Others of iron and steel.
They hammer and saw, they chisel and weld,
But someday their structures will fall.

But you, dear friend, build bridges of clay,
From one human life to another.
Your work is built on the Word of God
And nothing, no nothing, can sever!

My tribute to you (and it comes from my heart),
Is respect and admiration.
My praise to my God for a friend so true.....
My joy beyond explanation.

"Get all the wisdom you can and be wise the rest of your life."
Proverbs 19:20

1988

Gifts From A Loving Heart

Today we're thinking of you in a very special way.
Sending our congratulations on your anniversary day.

What can we give to ones so dear to help them celebrate
The love they share between them. Our son and his lovely mate.

We thought of buying candles to help brighten up your days,
Instead we're sending Prayers to help guide you on your way.

We thought of lovely roses in a priceless, ornate vase.
Instead we're asking God to give His Mercy and His Grace.

We could send you money for a gift or two.
Instead we're sending Support and Encouragement too.

A gift certificate would be real nice
But we would rather send Love which has no price.

Our Pride, Respect and Admiration…..our Joy beyond compare.
These are the gifts from our loving hearts, for your loving hearts to share.

"….for the message to us from the beginning has been that we should love one another."
I John 3:11

1975

The Gift Of Love

The Lord sent two angels to our home one day,
To love and encourage and show me the way.

My heart is so full….it's hard to express
What lies deep within and brings happiness.

But I know that somehow the love of true friends,
Is the gift that my Savior so freely extends.

For when I was hurting He knew and He cared.
The burden was lifted as with me you shared.

I asked and He answered. His word is still true.
My faith has grown stronger because He sent me you.

The gift I would give you each day of the year,
Is the gift of my friendship because you're so dear.

"God showed how much He loved us by sending His only Son
into this wicked world to bring to us eternal life through His death.
Ist John 4:9

1992

Our Greatest Friend

Her presence makes me happy.
Her kindness brings a smile.
When I need someone to talk to.
It's her number I will dial.
She's there when every things all right.
She's there when things go wrong.
She'll be there anytime at all.
Her love is deep and strong.
Sometimes I might be feeling blue.
My eyes are filled with tears.
Somehow she always seems to know,
And quiets all my fears.
And when I'm bubbling over
With happiness so sweet
She comes and shares my happy heart,
And makes me feel so neat.
She writes and calls and gives me gifts,
And wants to be with me.
Her thoughtful deeds express her love.
It's very plain to see.
I'm sure the Lord has blessed your life,
The way that He's blessed mine,
With friends who share your every care;
With whom your heart entwines.
But, if you have no friend on earth,
Remember this one thing……
Jesus is your greatest friend.
He'll make your sad heart sing.

*"I demand that you love each other as much as I love you.
And here is how to measure it-- the greatest love is shown when a person
lays down his life for his friends;
and you are my friends, if you obey me."*
John 15:12-14Ist John 4:9

Dear Reader,

From the young age of 22, my daily walk with the Lord has instilled. a willingness to listen to Him and be encouraged by His Word, no matter the circumstance or location. When I go for walks, hear the birds singing, sit by a babbling brook, or quietly meditate, I can hear the Lord whisper "write this down." For some time, I thought these messages that He placed on my heart were just for me. Then came the day when I knew He wanted me to share them with you. In sharing, my passion is to encourage your heart with words that have strengthened my life in order that you can embrace the Master Heartmender as well.

Often, good things which we celebrate come after the prod of a life-changing needle; every good thing in which we participate has a thread connecting directly back to God. When needle and thread connect, we can be assured that the Heartmender's work is underway.

In times of trials, have you ever wondered who and what to believe? In challenging times, these poems have inspired hope and strengthened my faith. They have brought peace, joy, and comfort and been a blessing to my family and friends. For ease of reference, the poems are organized into three groups, "Faith" Family" and "Friends". "Faith" will help you in your search for the true answers to life's questions. Perhaps you are looking for the reason for your existence. In Psalm 139, I discovered that I was deliberately formed by the hand of God. "You made all the delicate, inner parts of my body....and knit them together in my mother's womb"..."You saw me before I was born and scheduled each day of my life before I began to breathe. Every day was recorded in your book!" How these words encouraged my heart and showed me that I am not here by accident, but by the plan of God, to carry out His purpose. "He knows everything about me, even when I sit or stand. He knows my every thought. He even charts the path ahead of me and tells me when to stop and rest." What comfort! And He will do the same for you.

Section two is "Family". Just my way to let those I love know the impact they have had on my life. Perhaps you feel the same. Ephesians

3:14, 15 says "When I think of the wisdom and scope of His plan I fall down on my knees and pray to the Father of all the great family of God--some of them already in heaven and some down here on earth."

Families owe to God their existence with the opportunity and privilege of bearing distinctive names. As such each family member is required to follow God's standards...whether he is the head of the family, a mother, or children.

Here are some roles that are to be done by each member as set by the Bible.

Husbands: That is how husbands should treat their wives, loving them as parts of themselves. For since a man and his wife are now one, a man is really doing himself a favor and loving himself when he loves his wife! Ephesians 5:28-30.

Wives: So again I say, a man must love his wife as a part of himself; and the wife must see to it that she deeply respects her husband--obeying, praising and honoring him. Ephesians 5:33.

Marriage Mates: Honor your marriage and its vows, and be pure; for God will surely punish all those who are immoral or commit adultery. Hebrews 13:4

As Parents: Teach a child to choose the right path, and when he is older he will remain upon it. Proverbs 22:6

Children: Children, obey your parents; this is the right thing to do because God has placed them in authority over you. Ephesians 6:1

Section three is dedicated to Friends that have been there for me along my journey and the blessings each one has given. To all others, I consider each one of you a friend I haven't met yet, but look forward, with hope, that one day we we will.

In the Bible, you will find that Jesus is the reason to live. He will give you hope for the future. He is my Heartmender, and I know if you ask Him, He will become your Heartmender, too.